For Gregor

First published 2021 by Walker Books Ltd, 87 Vauxhall Walk, London SE11 5HJ

10 9 8 7 6 5 4 3 2 1

Text and illustrations © 2021 Catherine Rayner

The right of Catherine Rayner to be identified as author and illustrator of this work has been asserted by her in accordance with the Copyright, Designs and Patents Act 1988

This book has been typeset in Times New Larson and Triplex Serif

Printed in China

British Library Cataloguing in Publication Data: a catalogue record for this book is available from the British Library

ISBN 978-1-4063-8578-6

www.walker.co.uk

My pet GOLDFISH

Catherine Rayner

WALKER BOOKS
AND SUBSIDIARIES
LONDON · BOSTON · SYDNEY · AUCKLAND

WHEN I was four, I got my first ever pet: a fish
no bigger than my hand, with red and orange scales.

My very own goldfish!

He didn't have a name yet,

so I got to choose one —

and I called him "Richard".

7

Richard went to live in the big tank in our kitchen, with all my sister's fish. There were lots of plants for him to nibble, rocks for him to suck and pebbles to search through for bits of food.

Goldfish have been kept
as pets for thousands
of years.

Goldfish need plenty
of space to grow properly, so
you need a BIG tank to keep them in.

After school, I would tell Richard about my day. He would swim over when he saw me, wiggling his tail; if I gently touched the glass, he would follow my finger.

People think goldfish forget things quickly, but that can't be right – because Richard definitely knew who I was.

Scientists believe goldfish can remember things for up to five months.

Goldfish have very good eyesight — they can see even more colours than humans.

One day,
my friend Sandy
came over to meet
Richard. Sandy lives
next door and he knows
a LOT about fish.

Richard was hiding —
at first we couldn't see
where. Then we spotted him...

"When he's still," Sandy told me,

"that means he's having a nap — even though

his eyes look open. That's 'cause fish don't have eyelids."

Goldfish don't have
lungs like we do —
they breathe using gills.

Goldfish use their eyesight
and sense of smell to find food.

Richard seemed to hear Sandy – he swam up
to the surface and started blowing bubbles.

"He does that when he's hungry," I said, and gave him some fish
flakes. "He likes eating these – but worms are his favourite."
"Worms?" said Sandy. He sounded impressed. "I wonder
if my fish like worms."

A group of goldfish is
called a "troubling".

16

Sandy showed me the pond in his garden – it was full of goldfish!

They wiggled and whirled through the water, their scales shining. These fish were MUCH bigger than Richard.

I looked closely. There were some tiny
grey fish, too – the size of dots.

"Look at those ones," I said, pointing.

"Those are the babies," said Sandy. "Their
scales will get brighter as they grow up."

Baby goldfish
are called
"fry".

Sandy's fish were all different shapes, sizes and
colours – there was even one that looked
like it was wearing goggles!

"That one's a 'telescope' goldfish," Sandy told me. "She's very fancy."

There are over two hundred different kinds of goldfish.

Different species include "comets", "Shubunkins", "bubble-eyes", "butterfly tails", "pompoms"!

A fish swam up to us – it was

HUGE, nearly as long as my arm!

"This is Goldy," said Sandy. "He's eighteen…

Even older than my brother."

"Richard's only two," I said, frowning.

"But if he gets as big as Goldy, he won't fit in our tank."

"That's OK," Sandy told me. "Then he can live in

our pond – and you can see him all the time."

I liked the sound of that:

Richard would have a lot

of space for swimming,

and new friends too.

The oldest ever goldfish
was 43 years old.

Richard grew ...

and grew ...

and grew...

When he was four-and-a-half,
he was finally ready to live in
Sandy's beautiful pond.

Goldfish can grow to be up to 30 cm long.

25

I go and see him all the time. I sit by the edge of the pond and he swims up, doing the same happy little dance and wiggling his tail ... as if to say "Remember me?"

NOTE FROM THE AUTHOR

The Richard in this story is named after my real goldfish — and he's full of character!

I've had goldfish nearly all my life: they make very good pets.
If you decide to get a fish of your own, here are a few tips.

YOUR FISH WILL NEED:

o A very large tank to live in, with a filter and an air pump.* You also need to clean the glass every now and then.

o Some good-quality goldfish food.

o Lots of interesting plants, gravel and hiding places.
   (But remember to leave enough space for them to swim about happily with their fishy friends!)

o About a fifth of the water in the tank needs changing regularly, and treating with special drops from your pet shop.**
   (Tap water has a chemical called "chlorine" in it, which is dangerous for your fish.)

* Goldfish "bowls" don't make good homes for fish, as they are normally too small.

** Remember to let the new water sit in a bucket near your tank for at least 15 minutes before you pour it in, so it's the same temperature as the rest — not too hot and not too cold.

INDEX

To Find Out More

I very much recommend *How to Look After Your Goldfish*
by David Alderton, and the website: **thegoldfishtank.com**